THE BIG BOOK of
CRACK YOURSELF UP
JOKES FOR KIDS

Other Books by Sandy Silverthorne

Crack Yourself Up Jokes for Kids
More Crack Yourself Up Jokes for Kids
Made You Laugh!
Now That's Funny

THE BiG BOOK of CRACK YOURSELF UP

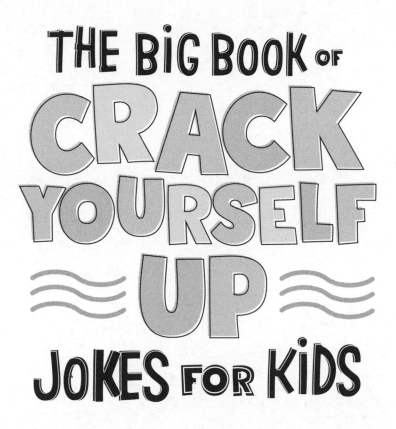

JOKES FOR KiDS

SANDY SiLVERTHORNE

Revell

a division of Baker Publishing Group
Grand Rapids, Michigan

© 2018, 2019 by Sandy Silverthorne

Published by Revell
a division of Baker Publishing Group
PO Box 6287, Grand Rapids, MI 49516-6287
www.revellbooks.com

Combined edition published 2021
ISBN 978-0-8007-4051-1 (paper)
ISBN 978-0-8007-4123-5 (casebound)

Previously published in two separate volumes:
Crack Yourself Up Jokes for Kids © 2018
More Crack Yourself Up Jokes for Kids © 2019

Printed in the United States of America

The author is represented by WordServe Literary Group www.wordserveliterary.com.

21 22 23 24 25 26 27   7 6 5 4 3 2 1

Do you like to crack your friends up? Do you like to crack your parents up? How about your teachers? Your brothers and sisters? Most of all, do you like to crack *yourself* up? Then you came to the right place. This fun, crazy joke book is filled with the greatest jokes, stories, knock knocks, and riddles in the world.

It's also got some really nutty cartoons to go along with them. So get to it. Get ready to read. Get ready to chuckle. And get ready to crack yourself up!

CRACK YOURSELF UP

JOKES FOR KIDS

Q: What musical instrument is found in the bathroom?

A: A tuba toothpaste.

Q: What's red and smells like blue paint?

A: Red paint.

Q: What kind of lights did Noah use on the ark?

A: Flood lights.

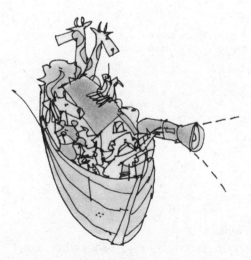

Q: Where do pencils go on vacation?

A: Pencilvania.

Q: What did the janitor say when he jumped out of the closet?

A: SUPPLIES!

SUPPLIES!

Q: What did the ocean say to the shore?

A: Nothing; it just waved.

Q: What do porcupines say when they kiss?

A: Ouch.

If Ella from *Ella Enchanted* married Darth Vader would she be Ella Vader?

Mason: How can you make sure you never wake up sleepy and grumpy?

Jason: Don't have a sleepover with the Seven Dwarfs.

Bill: My grades are underwater.

Phil: What do you mean?

Bill: They're below C level.

Terry: When they built the Great Wall of China, where did the workers go for supplies?

Jerry: Wal-Mart, of course.

If Cardinal Sicola were to become the pope, would he be Pope Sicola?

Q: What did the hamburger name his daughter?

A: Patty.

Jim: Why do birds fly south for the winter?
Tim: It's so much faster than walking.

Q: What do Alexander the Great and Winnie the Pooh have in common?

A: Same middle name.

Q: What do you call a pile of kittens?

A: A meowtain.

Q: What's red and goes up and down?

A: A tomato in an elevator.

Did you hear about the corduroy pillows?
They're making headlines.

Little Girl: Mommy, you've got some gray hairs.

Mom: Yes, every time you don't behave, I get another gray hair.

Little Girl: Is that why Grandma has so many?

Ron: Come see this photo of my aunt.

Don: That's a picture of a fish!

Ron: I know. It's my anchovy!

Teacher: Samuel, use the word *boycott* in a sentence.

Samuel: The boycott four fish and his sister only caught three.

Teacher: Sophie, use the word *information* in a sentence.

Sophie: Ducks fly information when they're heading south.

A guy walks into a lawyer's office and asks what he charges.

"I charge $1,000 for three questions," the lawyer answered.

"Wow, that's pretty expensive isn't it?" the man said.

"Yes it is," said the lawyer. "What's your third question?"

I couldn't believe it when the Highway Department called my dad a thief. But when I got home all the signs were there.

Knock, knock.

Who's there?

Lettuce.

Lettuce who?

Lettuce in! We're freezing out here!

Knock, knock.

Who's there?

Pizza.

Pizza who?

Pizza really great guy, don't you think?

Knock, knock.

Who's there?

Dishes.

Dishes who?

Dishes your father speaking. Open the door!

Man: Doctor, you've got to help me. I'm convinced
I'm a cocker spaniel.

Psychiatrist: Come in and lie down on the couch.

Man: I can't. I'm not allowed on the furniture!

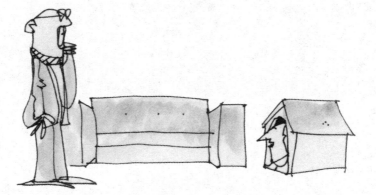

Q: Why did the skeleton stay home from the dance?

A: Because he had no-body to go with him.

Q: What music scares balloons?

A: Pop music.

Donny: So what are you doing today?
Lonny: Nothing.
Donny: Nothing? That's what you did all day yesterday.
Lonny: I know. I'm not finished yet.

Q: Why is England so wet?

A: Because the Queen has reigned there for years.

Q: Why did the lawyer bring a briefcase and a ladder to the courtroom?

A: He wanted to take his case to a higher court.

Braeden: I just got two cupcakes for my brother.

Caden: Wow, that was a good swap.

My doctor told me to play 18 holes every day.

So I took up the harmonica.

Did you hear about the missing barber?

Police are combing the city.

Len: I fell off a thirty-foot ladder yesterday.

Ben: Wow! Are you okay?

Len: Yeah, I was only on the second rung.

Knock, knock.

Who's there?

Radio.

Radio who?

Radio not, here I come!

Knock, knock.

Who's there?

Old Lady.

Old Lady who?

Wow, you can yodel!

Q: What kind of cars do kittens drive?

A: Catillacs.

Q: What did the judge say when the skunk walked in the courtroom?

A: Odor in the court.

Q: What goes "Tick Tick Woof Woof"?

A: A Watchdog.

Ed: Why did the soft drink can presser quit his job?

Ned: Because it was soda pressing.

Q: What has three letters and starts with gas?

A: A car.

Patient: Doctor, I feel like a butterfly.

Psychiatrist: Have you always felt this way?

Patient: No, a couple years ago I felt like a caterpillar.

Q: What do a dog and a telephone have in common?

A: Both have a collar ID.

Q: What do you call a dinosaur with a good vocabulary?

A: A Thesaurus.

Q: Why do seagulls fly over the sea?

A: Because if they flew over the bay they'd be called bagels!

Q: What did the lawyer name his daughter?

A: Sue.

Q: What do you get when you cross a rooster with a giraffe?

A: An animal who wakes people who live on the top floor.

Q: Why are dogs such bad dancers?

A: They have two left feet.

Diner: Waiter, do you have frog legs?

Waiter: Yes.

Diner: Then hop over here and take my order.

Diner: Waiter, what's this fly doing in my soup?

Waiter: It appears to be the backstroke.

Diner: Waiter, this soup is awful. Who made it?

Waiter: We all had a hand in it.

Joe: I went for seven days without sleep and I'm not even tired.

Flo: Wow! How did you do it?

Joe: I slept at night.

Diner: Waiter, how long have you worked here?

Waiter: Three months.

Diner: Oh, then you weren't the one who took my order.

Diner: Waiter, get your thumb off my waffles!

Waiter: And have them fall on the floor again?

Gladys: I keep seeing spots before my eyes.

Mabel: Have you seen a doctor?

Gladys: No, just these spots.

Boss: You made a fool out of me!

Worker: I can't take all the credit. You do a pretty good job yourself.

Q: Why did Tyler tiptoe past the medicine cabinet?

A: He didn't want to wake the sleeping pills!

A little boy went with his grandmother to his first ballet.

After watching the dancers on their toes for most of the performance, he turned to Grandma and said, "If they'd wanted taller dancers why didn't they just hire some?"

Man: Doctor, every time I drink a cup of coffee, I get a sharp pain in my eye.

Doctor: Try taking the spoon out before you drink it.

Diner: I refuse to eat this steak! Call the manager.

Waiter: It's no use. He won't eat it either.

Waiter: And how did you find your steak, sir?

Diner: Easy—I just moved the mashed potatoes and there it was!

A soccer player was yelling at his own goalie, "Why didn't you stop the ball?"

The goalie replied, "Excuse me. I thought that's what the net was for!"

Duchess: Will you join me in a cup of tea?
Duke: Do you think we can both fit?

Turkey Mom to her chick: You're behaving so badly, your father must be rolling over in his gravy!

Q: A box is filled with water and weighs 1,000 pounds. What can you add to it to make it lighter?

A: Holes.

Movie Theater Ticket Seller: Sir, that's the sixth ticket you've bought.

Moviegoer: I know. That guy by the rope keeps tearing them up.

Teacher: What did George Washington say after he crossed the Delaware River?

Jack: Everybody out of the boat!

Phil: My wife and I are going to the Caribbean.
Will: Jamaica?
Phil: No, she wanted to go.

Q: What happens to a frog who overparks?
A: He gets toad.

Ben: What's the difference between an elephant and a mailbox?
Len: I don't know.
Ben: Well, I'm not sending you to mail a letter.

Bill: Will you remember me in a day, a week, a month?
Jill: Absolutely. I'll never forget you.
Bill: Knock, knock.
Jill: Who's there?
Bill: You said you'd remember me!

Q: How does a mermaid call her friends?

A: On her shell phone.

Q: What's brown and sticky?

A: A stick.

Q: What do you call a polar bear wearing earmuffs?

A: Anything you want. He can't hear you!

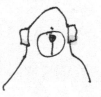

Hello? Can you hear me now?

Q: What do you call a belt made out of watches?

A: A waist of time.

Q: **How do you count cows?**

A: With a cowculator.

Q: **What kind of shoes do frogs wear?**

A: Open toad.

Peg: What is green and brown and crawls through the grass?

Meg: A Girl Scout who lost her cookie.

A man was talking to God one day.

"Lord, is it true that to you a million years is like a minute?"

"Yes, that's true."

"And a million dollars is like a penny?"

"Yes, that's true too."

The man hesitated. "Lord, will you give me a penny?"

"In a minute."

Mom: Why are you scratching yourself, Alfie?
Alfie: 'Cause no one else knows where I itch.

Mick: Did you know that deep breathing kills germs?
Dick: Yes, but how do I get them to breathe deeply?

A little girl was drawing a picture in her Sunday school class.

The teacher asked, "What are you drawing, Natalie?"

"I'm drawing a picture of God," she answered.

"But nobody knows what God looks like," the teacher said.

Natalie smiled and said, "They will in a minute."

Customer: Will the band play anything I ask them to?

Bandleader: Sure.

Customer: Then ask them to play chess.

Boss: What were you before you started working here?

Jamie: Happy.

Nate: My teacher was mad because I didn't know where the pyramids were.

Mom: Well, try to remember where you put things.

Salesman: This computer will do half your work
for you.

Customer: In that case, I'll take two.

Customer: I think I can put this wallpaper on myself.

Salesman: Go ahead, but most people prefer to put it on
the wall.

Susie was so excited that she put together a puzzle in just
10 days even though the box said 2–4 years.

Q: What do you get when you cross a stream and a brook?

A: Wet feet.

Teacher: "Whoever answers my next question can go home."

A boy throws his backpack out the window.

"Who threw that?" the teacher said.

"I did," the boy answered. "I'm going home."

A blonde yells to another blonde across the river, "How do I get to the other side?"

"You *are* on the other side!"

Q: Why was Cinderella thrown off the basketball team?

A: 'Cause she ran away from the ball.

In a school cafeteria there was a small sign that said, "Please take just one apple. God is watching."

At the end of the counter by the tray of cookies, someone had scribbled out another sign that said, "Take all the cookies you want. God is watching the apples."

Principal: Where were you born, son?

Tyler: In the United States.

Principal: Which part?

Tyler: All of me.

Kid: My dad's a magician. He saws people in half.

Syd: Wow. Do you have any siblings?

Kid: Three half sisters and a half brother.

Q: Why did the baby cookie cry?

A: Because his father was a wafer so long.

Q: What do ducks watch on TV?

A: Duckumentaries.

Teacher: In the Bible, Lot was told to take his wife and flee out of the city. His wife looked back and turned to salt.

Student: What happened to the flea?

Bill: Did you hear that Marvin got a job as a ditch digger?

Phil: Great. How did that happen?

Bill: He just fell into it.

Q: What do you call a guy lying on your doorstep?

A: Matt.

Knock, knock.

Who's there?

Stopwatch.

Stopwatch who?

Stopwatch you're doing and open the door!

Q: How do you keep a rhino from charging?

A: Take away his credit card.

Q: What washes up on tiny beaches?

A: Microwaves.

Q: When is it bad luck to have a black cat following you?

A: When you're a mouse.

Q: What do you call it when dinosaurs crash their cars?
A: Tyrannosaurus Wrecks.

Kyle stole the ketchup, but the cops caught him red-handed.

Q: Where do vegetables volunteer?
A: The Peas Corps.

Apparently I snore so loudly it scares all the people in the car I'm driving.

Q: What is heavy forward but not backward?

A: Ton.

Whenever I fill out an application, in the line that says who to contact in case of an emergency, I always write down "doctor."

Dolphins are so smart they teach people to stand by the pool and toss them fish.

Don: Why did the kid put a flashlight in his suit of armor?

Ron: He wanted to make a Knight-Light.

Rowan: Hey Ava, what do you say to a nice walk?

Ava: That sounds lovely.

Rowan: Good, will you pick me up some donuts and chips while you're out there?

Mack: According to statistics, a person is robbed in Chicago every seven minutes.

Mike: That poor guy should consider moving.

Tried to catch fog yesterday. Mist.

Q: What does a pirate who just turned 80 say?

A: Aye Matey!

Knock, knock.

Who's there?

Gorilla.

Gorilla who?

Gorilla me up a hamburger.

Knock, knock.

Who's there?

Amish.

Amish who?

Sweet, I miss you too.

Knock, knock.

Who's there?

Alex.

Alex who?

Alex the questions around here.

Q: What did the elevator say to the other elevator?

A: I think I'm coming down with something.

My favorite nation in the world? Donation! Give me 10 bucks.

Did you hear about the two guys who stole a calendar?
They each got six months.

Q: What do you call birds who stick together?

A: Velcrows.

Q: What's gray and can't fly?

A: A parking lot.

Coworker: Excuse me, can I disturb you for a second?

    Walt: Sure, what is it?

Coworker: Nothing. I just wanted to disturb you.

Chad: It's times like this I wish I'd listened to what my dad always said.

Rad: What did he say?

Chad: I don't know. I wasn't listening.

Q: What's white and sits on your TV?

A: A fly wearing a nightgown.

Q: What would happen if you threw blue tennies into the Red Sea?

A: They'd get wet.

Man: Please send the ambulance! My wife is having a baby!

Operator: Okay, calm down. Is this her first child?

Man: No, this is her husband!

Q: This guy shaves 15 times a day but still has a beard. How come?

A: He's a barber.

Diner: Waiter, I can't possibly eat all this. Could I have a doggy bag to take it home?

Waiter: Sir, this is the buffet table.

Officer: Your driver's license, please.

Susie: So sorry, I forgot.

Officer: At home?

Susie: No, to get one.

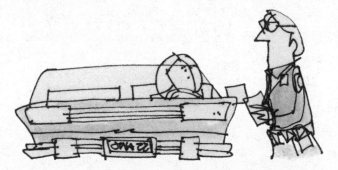

My teacher told me to have a good day, so I went home.

Did you hear about the guy who made a photocopy then compared it to the original to make sure there were no spelling errors?

Candy: Did you have any trouble with the test questions?
Andy: Not at all. It was the answers that were
a pain.

The main reason for a child's middle name—
so he can tell when he's really in trouble.

Did you hear about the popcorn truck accident at the army base?
Three kernels were lost.

Max: Grandma, how old are you?
Grandma: 39 and holding.
Max: How old would you be if you let go?

Q: What did one plate say to the other one?

A: Dinner's on me!

Q: What sport do you play with a wombat?

A: Wom, of course.

Teacher: Sam, what two days of the week start with T?

Sam: Today and Tomorrow!

Q: What did the tie say to the hat?

A: You go on a head. I'll just hang around.

Q: Why is the math book so sad?

A: Because it's got so many problems.

Madame: Why didn't you water the plants yesterday?
  Jeeves: It was raining, ma'am.
Madame: Don't make excuses. You could have used an
  umbrella.

Q: What's green and sings?

A: Elvis Parsley.

I'd like to get a job cleaning mirrors.
  It's really something I could see myself doing.

A guy discovered four penguins wandering around his backyard.

His neighbor peeked over the fence and said, "What have you got there?"

"Some penguins. I don't know where they came from."

"You should take them over to the zoo."

"Good idea." So he loaded them into the back of his pickup.

The next day the neighbor saw the man loading the penguins into his pickup truck again.

"I thought you were taking those birds to the zoo."

"I did. We had such a nice time that today we're going to Disney World."

A mom texts her son: What do IDK, LY, and
TTYL mean?

    Son: I Don't Know, Love You, and Talk to
You Later.

    Mom: Okay. I'll try asking someone else.

Brian: My uncle is a big shot. He's got 3,000 people
under him.

    Ryan: Is he a CEO?

Brian: No, he cuts the grass in a cemetery.

    Tad: What does a clock do when it's hungry?

    Rad: It goes back four seconds.

**Q: If cakes are 66 cents each, how much are upside-down
cakes?**

A: 99 cents.

Q: What do you get if you cross an electric blanket with a toaster?

A: People who pop out of bed in the morning.

Health Inspector: I'm afraid you have too many roaches in here.

Restaurant Owner: How many am I allowed?

Q: Who isn't your brother or your sister but is still the child of your parents?

A: You.

Upset Patient: Doctor, I'm convinced I'm a pair of curtains.

Psychiatrist: Well stop complaining and pull yourself together.

Knock, knock.

Who's there?

Summons.

Summons who?

Summons at the door.

Jason is such a dummy that during a power failure at the mall, he got stuck on an escalator for two and a half hours.

Were you long in the hospital?

No, I was about the same size
as I've always been.

Lyle: Why did Sam leave his job?
Kyle: Illness.
Lyle: Really?
Kyle: Yeah, his boss got sick of him.

Man: Doctor, I'm convinced I'm a deck of cards.
Doctor: Wait here. I'll deal with you in a minute.

Boss: Look at this office. It looks like it hasn't been cleaned in over a month!
Gus: Don't blame me! I've only been here since Thursday.

I've been taking French lessons because we're adopting a baby from France. That way I'll be able to understand what he says when he starts talking.

Gladys: I made the chicken soup.

Chauncey: Thank goodness. I thought it was for us.

Remy: When is a car not a car?

Rowan: When it turns into a driveway.

Isabel: When is a door not a door?

Charlotte: When it's ajar.

Ron: Is this bug spray good for mosquitoes?
Jon: No way. It'll kill them.

Sal: You'd be a good dancer if it wasn't for two things.
Hal: What are those?
Sal: Your feet.

Bob: I have a photographic memory.
Rob: Too bad it never developed.

I'm reading a book about antigravity.
 I can't put it down.

There are only three kinds of people.
 Those who can count, and those who can't.

Christy: I lost my contact lens.

Misty: Where did you lose it?

Christy: Over by the bookcase.

Misty: Then why are you looking for it over here?

Christy: Because the light is so much better here.

Mom: Noah, why are you so upset?

Noah: I just got an invitation to a birthday party. It says 4–7 and I can't go 'cause I'm eight!

Singer: I take requests.

Diner: Good. Can you sing "Far, Far Away"?

Dad: How do you like school, Aiden?

Aiden: Closed.

Alex: Dad, would you do my math for me?

Dad: No, it wouldn't be right.

Alex: Oh, you don't understand it either?

Addie: My aunt's a kleptomaniac.

Abby: Is she taking anything for it?

I've told you a million times—don't exaggerate!

Girl: I'm tan from the sun.

Boy: Hi, I'm Jacob from the Earth.

Officer: How did you manage to crash your car?

Driver: See that telephone pole over there?

Officer: Yeah.

Driver: Well, I didn't.

"The horse I bet on was a real champion," the Texan bragged. "It took seven others to beat him."

Movie Star: My fan letters keep three secretaries busy.

Agent: Answering them?

Movie Star: No, writing them.

A young man came in to speak to the father of the girl he was planning to marry.

"Son, before you can marry my daughter, tell me—can you support a family?" the dad asked.

"I can support us," the young man answered, "but you're on your own."

Q: What dog do you find at an embassy?

A: A Diplomutt.

Q: Why did the clock get kicked out of class?

A: It tocked too much.

Jim: What has 18 legs and goes crunch, crunch, crunch?

Tim: A baseball team eating potato chips.

Q: What do you get when you cross the Invisible Man with an elephant?

A: A big nothing.

Ryan: Why are you moving to another state?

Brian: I read that 90 percent of accidents happen within five miles of your home.

Shopper: Do you have any loafers?

Shoe Store Clerk: We certainly do.

Shopper: Well, have one of them come over here and wait on me.

Grandpa: The town I grew up in was really small.

    Kid: How small was it?

Grandpa: Our zip code was a fraction.

Knock, knock.

Who's there?

Nod.

Nod who?

Nod you again.

Did you hear about the guy who swallowed a dictionary?

    He didn't breathe a word of it to anyone.

    Kid: Dad, will you buy me a drum set?

    Dad: Are you kidding? There's way too much noise
around here already.

    Kid: That's okay! I'll only practice when you're asleep.

Teacher: Do you think you can sleep in my class?

Student: I could if you wouldn't talk so loud.

Did you hear about the guy who kept a bicycle in his bedroom?

He was tired of walking in his sleep.

Teacher: David, what's another name for a bunch of bees?

David: A great report card!

Teacher: The law of gravity explains why we stay on the ground.

Student: How did we do it before the law was passed?

Lady: Hello, Fire Department? My garage is on fire!

Fireman: Okay, stay calm. How do we get there?

Lady: Oh, I think you should drive your big, red fire truck.

Diner: I'd like the special and coffee with no cream.

New Waitress: I'm sorry, we're out of cream. Would you like it with no milk instead?

Teacher: Joey, if you had twenty dollars in your front pocket, thirty dollars in your back pocket, and fifty dollars in your side pocket, what would you have?

Joey: Someone else's pants!

Jon: Why are you wearing those loud socks?

Ron: 'Cause my feet keep falling asleep.

Kylie: Why are you putting lipstick on your forehead?

Chloe: I'm trying to make up my mind.

Q: What do they call the time in history when nerds ruled the land?

A: The Dork Ages.

Q: How do you make antifreeze?

A: Take away her blanket.

Mrs. Bailey: My husband just got run over by a steamroller! What should I do?

Doctor: Tell him to lie flat on his back.

Josh: Dad, I lost my pet snake.

Dad: You need to put up signs around the neighborhood.

Josh: That won't help—he can't read.

Knock, knock.

Who's there?

Althea.

Althea who?

Althea later, alligator.

Mom: How was your first day of school, Danny?

Danny: Oh, not so good. The teacher said, "Danny, I want you to sit here for the present." So I did. All day. And I never got the present!

Teacher: Have you ever traced your ancestors?

Asher: No, I'm not that good at drawing.

Q: What did the contractor say to the electrician when he arrived to the work site at noon?

A: Wire you insulate?

Bo: Why did Jimmy hit his head on the piano keys?

Jo: He was learning to play by ear.

Q: How do grizzlies like to walk on the beach?

A: Bearfoot.

A man went into the hospital for some tests. As he lay on the table, a big black Labrador came in the room and sniffed all around him. After he left, a cat came in and jumped up on the table and explored the guy from head to toe. When the man got home, he got a bill for $1,500.

"What was this for?" he exclaimed as he called the hospital.

"Oh," she said as she looked at the man's records, "that was for the Lab Test and the Cat Scan."

My parents always had to pay my brother to be good.

But not me—I was good for nothing!

Q: What's an alien's favorite snack?

A: Martian-mellows.

Q: What kind of music do planets listen to?

A: Neptunes.

Q: What kind of horses go out after dark?

A: Nightmares.

Q: What's a light-year?

A: A regular year but with fewer calories.

Q: Who's in charge of the pencil box?

A: The ruler!

Rowan: Why did Rose go out with her purse wide open?
Remy: She heard there was going to be some change in the weather.

Teacher: What happens when you touch a window?
Smart Kid: You feel the pane.

Farmer Brown: What do cows use in their text messages?

Mrs. Brown: E-moo-jis.

Doctor: There's good news and bad news. The good news is you're to take one of these pills a day for the rest of your life.

Patient: But there are only seven pills in here.

Doctor: That brings us to the bad news.

Q: What's black and white and eats like a horse?

A: A zebra.

Q: What is the Tower of Pisa's first name?

A: Eileen.

Mike: Why did the chicken cross the road?
  Ike: To see the dumb guy.
Mike: Knock, knock.
  Ike: Who's there?
Mike: The chicken.

Teacher: Timmy, what did you write your report on?
Timmy: A piece of paper.

Knock, knock.

Who's there?

Mikey.

Mikey who?

Mikey doesn't work. Will you open the door?

Deagan: Why did the man put bandages in his refrigerator?
Hannah: He wanted some cold cuts.

Q: What kind of pig likes to drive a car?
A: A road hog.

Q: Why didn't the sun go to grad school?

A: 'Cause it already had a million degrees.

Q: What becomes shorter when you add two letters to it?

A: Short.

Q: What did the duck say when he bought lip balm?

A: Just put it on my bill.

Q: How do lumberjacks get onto the internet?

A: They log in.

Two brothers, Jamie and Sam, were deciding who got to eat the last waffle. Mom came in and suggested, "Boys, don't you think Jesus would want you to share? I think he would give his waffle to his brother."

"That's a good idea," Sam said. "Jamie, you be Jesus."

Math Teacher: If you have 10 apples in one hand and 13 oranges in your other hand, what do you have?

Thomas: Big hands!

Teacher: James, where was the Constitution of the United States signed?

James: At the bottom!

Aiden: Why did Grandma put roller skates on her rocking chair?

Caden: 'Cause she wanted to rock and roll.

Knock, knock.

Who's there?

Samurai.

Samurai who?

Samurai will pick you up after school.

Knock, knock.

Who's there?

Butter.

Butter who?

Butter come over here and answer the door!

Q: Why is a river so rich?

A: Because it has two banks.

Q: Where does a track and field athlete keep his money?

A: In the pole vault.

Q: Where do pigs go on sunny Saturdays?

A: Pignics.

> **Max:** Can you help me? I'm looking for where I can get an ark.
>
> **Jax:** Oh, I Noah guy.

On a huge sailing ship the galley master went below deck and addressed the men who were rowing in the hull.

> **Galley Master:** I've got good news and bad news. The good news is there will be more food rations tonight!
>
> **Men:** Hooray! What's the bad news?
>
> **Galley Master:** The captain wants to go water skiing.

FASTER!

Q: What is a mummy's favorite kind of music?

A: Wrap music, of course.

Knock, knock.

Who's there?

Nunya.

Nunya who?

Nunya business.

Knock, knock.

Who's there?

Kent.

Kent who?

Kent you tell? I'm standing right here!

Q: Where do cows go on a date?

A: To the moo-vies.

Knock, knock.

Who's there?

Harry.

Harry who?

Harry up and open the door!

Knock, knock.

Who's there?

Justin.

Justin who?

Justin time to tell you another knock-knock joke.

Mr. Anderson: Were any famous men or women born on
           your birthday?
           Joey: No, only little babies.

Q: Why did the baby join the army?

A: He wanted to be in the *infant*ry.

Patient: Doctor, you've got to help me. I think I'm losing my memory. I can't remember anything!

Doctor: How long have you had this problem?

Patient: What problem?

Q: What does the razor put in his coffee?

A: Shaving cream.

Teacher: James, how do you spell *crocodile*?

James: K-R-O-C-I-D-I-L-E.

Teacher: That's wrong.

James: Maybe, but you asked me how *I* spell it.

Teacher: Sammie, name one great thing that we have today
that we didn't have 10 years ago.

Sammie: Me!

Policeman: I'm sorry, but your truck is way too
overloaded. I'm going to need to take your
license.

Truck Driver: Oh that won't help. It can't weigh more than
two or three ounces.

Q: What's an ant's favorite country?

A: Frants.

Aiden was playing ball in his aunt's house when he missed and broke the vase that was on the mantle.

"Do you realize that vase was from the seventeenth century?" his aunt said. "It was over 300 years old!"

"Oh whew," Aiden said, "I was afraid it was new."

Q: What did one candle say to the other?

A: I'm going out tonight.

Q: What do you call a sleeping bull?

A: A bulldozer.

BACKWARD JOKES

Backward jokes give the answer first, then the question. Here's an example:

The answer is Kitty Litter.

The question is, What does Garfield throw out the car window?

Answer: Cyclone.

Question: What do you call a clone of a guy named Cy?

Answer: Supervisor.

Question: What does Superman wear to keep the sun out of his eyes?

Answer: Rose Bowl.

Question: What do you say when it's Rose's turn at the bowling alley?

Answer: Catch-22.

Question: What does a terrible baseball team do with 100 fly balls?

I GOT IT!!!

Answer: Mount Rushmore.

Question: What do you need to do to ride your horse named Rushmore?

Answer: Defense.

Question: What's between your and da neighbor's yard?

Answer: Despair.

Question: What are you glad you have in case of a
flat tire?

Answer: Timbuktwo.

Question: What comes after Timbuk one?

Answer: Hoe Down.

Question: What does the farmer do when he's done working
for the day?

Answer: Egg White.

Question: What is the name of Snow White's first child?

Knock, knock.

Who's there?

Wooden shoe.

Wooden shoe who?

Wooden shoe like to know.

Q: How do astronauts keep in touch with each other?

A: Spacebook.

Knock, knock.

Who's there?

Rita.

Rita who?

Rita book, and stop watching TV!

Knock, knock.

Who's there?

Jenny.

Jenny who?

Jenny'd to open the door right now!

I went to a massage therapist, but I've stopped going.
They rubbed me the wrong way.

Q: What time do ducks get up?

A: At the quack of dawn.

Q: Where do young tigers swim?

A: In the kitty pool.

Q: What do you get when you cross cocoa with a herd of cows?

A: Chocolate Moos.

Q: What can you hold without touching it?

A: A conversation.

Q: Why did the secret agent keep saying "1, 2, 3, 4, 5, 6, 7"?

A: He was a counterspy.

Why did you ask me to work out with you?

My doctor told me to
exercise with dumbbells.

Q: What does a bee use to cut wood?

A: A buzz saw.

Q: What's a polar bear's favorite game?

A: Freeze tag.

Q: What does a firefly order in a restaurant?

A: A light meal.

Alsea: Why do you have that lampshade on your head?

Max: I was feeling lightheaded.

Q: Why did the policeman open a bakery?

A: He wanted to make copcakes.

Q: What has four wheels and honks?

A: A goose on a skateboard.

Q: Who invented the telephone and carries your luggage?

A: Alexander Graham Bellhop.

Q: What does a dog take on a camping trip?

A: A pup tent.

She loved the pastry chef, but always feared he'd dessert her.

It was Daddy's turn to read bedtime stories to his four-year-old son.

After about 20 minutes, Mom called up the stairs: "Is he asleep?"

The little boy answered, "Yes, finally."

Randy: What's black and white and red all over?

Andy: A panda eating chili without utensils.

Jason: What do you get when you cross an honor student with a giraffe?

Mason: A kid everyone can look up to.

Pat: Why can't you ever borrow money from a leprechaun?

Matt: 'Cause they're always a little short.

Q: When is a running boy not a boy?

A: When he's ahead in the race.

Logan: Ever see an egg roll?

Rogan: No, but I've seen an apple turnover.

Teacher: Conner, use the word *contrive* in a sentence.

Conner: When I get my license I contrive.

Knock, knock.

Who's there?

Avenue.

Avenue who?

Avenue knocked on this door before?

Bo: I just read the weather forecast for Baja, California.
Jo: What is it?
Bo: Chili today and hot tamale.

Q: What's gray, has 400 feet, and never leaves the ground?

A: A plane full of elephants.

Q: What do you call a fly with no wings?

A: A walk.

Q: What bug is on the ground but also a hundred feet in the air?

A: A centipede on his back.

Q: When should you buy a bird?

A: When it's going cheep.

Q: What steals your stuff while you're in the bathtub?

A: A robber ducky.

Iris: Why did the spotted owl go to school?

Dad: I don't know. Why?

Iris: He wanted to study owlgebra.

Mom (on the first day of school): What did you learn today, Andy?

Andy: Not enough, apparently—they want me to come back tomorrow.

Teacher: Does anyone know who broke the sound barrier?

Manny: Don't ask me. I'm no tattletale.

Q: Why did the student bring his artist pad to the political speech?

A: He wanted to draw his own conclusions.

Q: What has a foot on each end and a foot in the middle?

A: A yardstick.

Q: Where do bunnies get their eyes checked?

A: At the hoptometrist.

Teacher: Lucas, when I was your age I could do any math problem given to me.

Lucas: Yes, but you had a different teacher.

A dad and his son were out driving.

Dad: Oh no! I just went through that stop sign.

Son: Don't worry. The police car behind us did the same thing.

Robert: Do you want me to cut the pie into six pieces?
Grandma: Oh no. I could never eat six. Cut it into four.

Jan: My alarm clock went off at six this morning.
Dan: Did it ever come back?

Q: Did you hear about the acrobat who fell in love?
A: He was head over heels.

Don: I'm reading some books on plants.
Ron: Botany?
Don: No, I got them from the library.

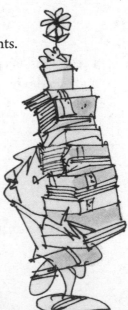

Jo: Is it true you always answer one question with another?

Bo: Who told you that?

Teacher: Jack, name two pronouns.

Jack: Who, me?

Teacher: Correct.

Q: Why did the millionaire never take a bath?

A: He wanted to be filthy rich.

I've been asking people what time it is since this morning, and everybody I ask tells me something different!

Mikey: Can you write in the dark, Dad?

Dad: I guess. What do you want me to write?

Mikey: Your name on this report card.

Peg: I can watch the sun rise from my bedroom.

Meg: So what? From my family room, I can watch the kitchen sink.

Bill: I used to wake myself up snoring.

Phil: What did you do to fix it?

Bill: Now I sleep in the other room.

Teacher: Stop acting like a fool!

Student: Who's acting?

Logan: Your problem is you're always wishing for something you don't have.

Rogan: Well, what else is there to wish for?

Diner: Waiter, this coffee tastes like mud.

Waiter: Well, it was ground this morning.

Todd: My great-great-grandfather fought with Napoleon, my grandfather fought with the British, and my father fought with the Americans.

Tad: Boy, your family can't get along with anybody.

Teacher: If you have five dollars and ask your father for five more, how much money would you have?

Sam: Five dollars.

Teacher: Boy, you don't know your math.

Sam: You don't know my father.

Hal: I'm back, and I've changed my mind.

Sal: Good. Does it work any better now?

Boss: What? Do you think I'm a perfect dummy?

Worker: Nonsense. Nobody's perfect.

Denny: What's the best way to prevent diseases caused by biting insects?

Penny: Don't bite any.

Phil: I swallowed a clock last week.

Doctor: Why didn't you tell me sooner?

Phil: I didn't want to alarm anybody.

Toby: Teacher, would you punish me for something I didn't do?

Teacher: No, of course not.

Toby: Good. I didn't do my homework.

Doctor: Have your eyes been checked lately?

Caleb: No, they've always been solid brown.

Mom: Did you take a bath today?

Lucas: Why? Is one missing?

Mom: Eric, wake up! It's twenty to nine!

Eric: In whose favor?

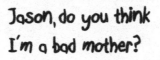

Jason, do you think
I'm a bad mother?

My name is Mark.

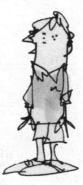

Josh is such a diligent student that last week he stayed up all night studying for a blood test.

Kid: Show me a tough kid, and I'll show you a big coward.

Bully: I'm a tough kid!

Kid: Well, I'm a big coward.

Customer: Why is my pizza all squished?

Pizza Guy: You said you wanted it that way.

Customer: I did?

Pizza Guy: Yeah, you said to give you a pizza and step on it!

Knock, knock.

Who's there?

Juicy.

Juicy who?

Juicy that shooting star?

Q: Where do cats go on vacation?

A: Meowmi Beach.

Q: Where do skunks sit in church?

A: In the pews.

Patient: Doctor, I still feel like I'm a worm. I'm not going to pay your bill.

Doctor: Oh yeah? You're not going to wiggle out of this one.

Q: What flies around the school at night?

A: An Alphabat.

Math Teacher: Jimmy, if you worked nine hours a day for a dollar an hour, what would you get?

Jimmy: A new job.

Chloe: What kind of shirts do army artillerymen wear?

Kylie: Tank tops!

She loved her earthquake scientist despite his faults.

Lon: What do wolves gargle with?

Don: Wolverine!

Salesman: This refrigerator will pay for itself in no time.

Customer: Good, send it over when it does.

This guy is so silly, he got water skis for his birthday.
Now he's looking for a lake with a hill in it.

Johnny: Mom, may I join the track team?

Mom: Run that by me again.

Max: When I was a child my babysitter dropped me
a lot.

Jax: What did your mom do?

Max: She got me a shorter babysitter.

Mrs. Inverness: Do you have any great-grandchildren?

Mrs. Iverson: No, they're all pretty average.

Leon: Bob, have you seen Harvey?

Bob: Yeah, he's round in front.

Leon: I know what he looks like. I'm asking where he is.

Ron: My grandma fell down the stairs.

Jon: Cellar?

Ron: No, I think she can be repaired.

I'm so broke I can't even pay attention!

Man: Hello, how much for a room?

Hotel Clerk: $150 a night.

Man: Do you take children?

Hotel Clerk: No, just cash or credit cards.

District Attorney: The court can produce dozens of witnesses who saw you rob that bank.

Criminal: So what? I can produce hundreds who didn't see me do it.

Customer: Buddy, will my pizza be long?
Pizza Guy: No, it'll be round just like all the others.

I've been reading article after article about how eating junk food is bad for you, so I made a New Year's resolution. From now on, no reading!

Growing up, our house was so small the mice were all hunchbacked.

Our house was so small that if you put the key in the front door, you broke the back window!

Q: What did William Shakespeare use when he got a flat?
A: His Shake-spare tire.

Q: What do you call an optometrist in the Aleutian islands?

A: An Optical Aleutian.

Customer: Have you got any kittens going cheap?
Pet Store Owner: No ma'am, all our kittens go meow.

Meow Meow Meow   CHEEP

The teacher pointed at me with a ruler and said, "At the end of this ruler is a real dunce!"

I got sent to the principal's office when I said, "Which end?"

Q: What did the baseball glove say to the baseball?

A: Catch you later!

Q: Where do TVs go on vacation?

A: To remote places.

Emily Biddle's Library of Book Titles:

Librarian Emily Biddle has a collection of unusual books in her bookmobile. Check out some of these titles:

Wiring Your House by Alec Tricity

The Sinking of the Titanic by Mandy Lifeboats

The History of Russia by Warren Peace

Not a Guitar! by Amanda Lynn

What Is Lunch? by Amelia Eat

The Unknown Rodent by A. Nonnie Mouse

I'm Fine by Howard Yu

Learn Sky Diving by Hugh First

Police Story by Laura Norder

How to Annoy People by Ann Tagonize

More Emily Biddle Book Titles:

Here are a few more interesting book titles from Emily's bookmobile:

Pick Up That Penny! by Ben Dover

Strong Breezes by Gustav Wind

Why Christy Walked to School by Mr. Buss

Taking a Quick Shower by I. C. Coldwater

Why Won't My Car Run? by M. T. Tank

Let Me In! by Isadore There

What's That in the Swamp? by Allie Gator

Introduction to Arithmetic by Adam Upp

The Empty House by Annie Buddyhome

Coming In First by Adam Myway

MORE CRACK YOURSELF UP JOKES FOR KIDS

Q: How does the Man in the Moon give himself a haircut?

A: Eclipse it.

Q: What did the mom broom say to the baby broom?

A: "Time to go to sweep, dear."

Q: What has four wheels and gives milk?

A: A cow on a skateboard.

Q: Why is a bee's hair always sticky?

A: Because they use honeycombs!

Q: Why did the man keep running around his bed?

A: Because he was trying to catch up on his sleep!

Caden: Will this road take me to Springfield?

Max: Nope. You're going to have to drive yourself.

Lonny: What's a runner's favorite subject in school?

Donny: Jog-raphy.

Q: What did the book name his daughter?

A: Page.

Christy: What is a kitten's favorite movie?

Misty: *The Sound of Mewsic.*

Q: What has four legs and flies?

A: Two birds.

Q: You break it every time you say it. What is it?

A: Silence.

Q: Where do whales go to hear music?

A: To the orca-stra!

Okay, once more from the top.

Q: Where do sheep go on vacation?

A: To the Baa-hamas.

Joe: What has four eyes but can't see?
Bo: Mississippi.

Jon: What can you catch but can't ever throw?

Ron: A cold.

Dan: What do you call a cow who cuts your grass?

Jan: A lawn mooer.

Brian: Where's a good place to store your dog?

Ryan: In the barking lot.

Patient: Doctor, I have a ringing in my ears. What should I do?

Doctor: Get an unlisted number.

Peg: What is salty and delicious and flies to the moon?

Meg: A rocket chip!

Q: What's a dog's favorite breakfast?

A: Pooched eggs.

Two eggs Rover easy.

Q: What do fish take to stay healthy?

A: Vitamin Sea.

Q: What's black and white, black and white, black and white, and green?

A: Three skunks fighting over a pickle.

Max: What do you call a dog who loves having its hair washed?

Alsea: A shampoodle.

Chad: What's a dog's favorite kind of pizza?

Rad: Pupperoni.

Ed: What do military camels wear?

Ned: Camelflage.

Rowan: How many sheep do you need to make a sweater?
Remy: I don't know; none of my sheep can knit.

Ava: What creature is smarter than a talking parrot?
Isabelle: A spelling bee!

Knock, knock.
Who's there?
Oliver.
Oliver who?
Oliver sudden I don't feel so good.

Teacher: Alex, which months have 28 days?
Alex: All of them!

Braeden: What is a lumberjack's favorite month?
Caden: Septimmmberrr!

Q: What do a tomato and a bicycle have in common?

A: They both have handlebars. Except the tomato.

Fred: Where does an astronaut park the space shuttle?
Charlotte: At a parking meteor.

Q: What should you do when a bull charges you?

A: Pay him.

Q: What starts with *t*, ends with *t*, and is full of *t*?

A: A teapot.

Teacher: How many seconds are there in a year?
Smart Aleck: Twelve. January 2nd, February 2nd,
March 2nd . . .

Q: What does a gorilla use to fix the sink?

A: A monkey wrench.

Len: How did the giraffe do in his classes?

Ben: He got high honors.

Jack: What did the sun say to Mercury?

Zach: "Can you give me some space?"

Q: What's the only grade you can plant a flower in?

A: Kindergarden!

Q: What can you have in your pocket while your pocket's still empty?

A: A hole.

I stayed in a really old hotel last night. They sent me a wake-up letter.

Q: What starts with *p* and ends with *e* and has a thousand letters?

A: Post office.

Q: A man arrives in a small town on Friday. He stays three days, then leaves on Friday. How is this possible?

A: Friday is the name of his horse.

Q: What belongs to you but others use it much more than you?

A: Your name.

Q: **David's father has three sons: Snap, Crackle, and**
_____?

A: No, silly. David!

Tongue Twisters

A synonym for cinnamon is a cinnamon synonym.

The great Greek grape growers grow great Greek grapes.

Any noise annoys an oyster, but a noisy noise annoys an oyster more.

Growing gray goats graze great green grassy groves.

Sal: Did you hear about the amazing invention that allows people to see through walls?
Hal: What is it?
Sal: A window.

Q: **What is brown and has a head and a tail but no legs?**
A: A penny.

Q: Where do frogs fly their flags?

A: Up tadpoles.

Q: Why did the cow cross the road?

A: It was going to the moo-vies.

Mason: What did you find when you traced your family tree?

Jason: Termites.

Teacher: James, why is your homework in your father's handwriting?

James: I used his pen!

Teacher: Joey, could you please pay a little attention?

Joey: I'm paying as little as I can.

Teacher: Why are you so late this morning?

Whitney: The sign said, "School Ahead, Go Slow."

Ron: Why did the musician put his guitar in the refrigerator?

Jon: He wanted to play some cool music.

Teacher: Now, kids, when I ask this next question, I want you to answer at once. What is three plus two?

Class: At once!

Q: Why did the painting go to prison?

A: Because it was framed.

Q: What happens when a policeman goes to bed?

A: He becomes an undercover cop.

Q: Where do bulls put their messages?

A: On the bull-etin board.

Q: **What do you get when you cross a jet with a hamburger?**

A: Some very fast food.

Hal: What are the biggest ants in the world?
Sal: Eleph-ants.

Q: **Why do hummingbirds hum?**

A: They forgot the words!

Chloe: My aunt lost 10 pounds on her trip to London.
Kylie: Wow, how did she do that?
Chloe: She left her wallet on a bus.

Q: **What did one pencil say to the other pencil?**

A: "You're looking sharp."

Q: What did one genius say to the other genius?

A: "You're looking smart."

Q: What did one puzzle say to the other puzzle?

A: "You look put together."

Q: What did one dog say to the other dog?

A: "You look fetching."

Q: What did one track runner say to the other track runner?

A: "You look dashing."

Sandy: What did the beach say to the tide as it came in?
Sunny: "Long time, no sea."

Q: What did the bacon say to the tomato?
A: "Lettuce get together."

Jason: Why did the gardener plant money in the ground?
Mason: He wanted his soil to be rich.

Jen: Why did the robber take a bath?

Ben: He wanted to make a clean getaway.

Ben: What do you get when you cross a fish and an elephant?

Len: Swimming trunks.

Q: What kind of beans do llamas like?

A: Llama beans, naturally.

Randy: What do you call a chicken who wakes you up in the morning?

Andy: An alarm cluck.

Logan: What do you say when you lose a Wii game?

Rogan: "I want a Wii-match!"

Q: What do you get when you cross a cow and a duck?

A: Milk and quackers.

Q: Why did the golfer wear two pairs of pants?

A: In case he got a hole in one.

Donny: Why did the guy put a clock under his desk?
Lonny: Because he wanted to work overtime.

Q: What runs but never gets anywhere?

A: A refrigerator.

Q: What do you get when you cross a cat with a lemon?

A: A sour puss.

Q: Where do sheep go to get their hair cut?

A: To the baa-baa shop.

Q: Why did the M&M go to college?

A: He wanted to be a Smartie.

Q: Why did the tree go to the dentist?

A: It needed a root canal.

Q: What is one word that looks the same upside down?

A: SWIMS.

Patient: Doctor, I'm convinced I'm a pretzel.
Doctor: Don't worry. I'll straighten you out in no time.

Moo.

That's what I was going to say.

Stan: Did you hear the story about the broken pencil?

Dan: No.

Stan: Never mind. It's kind of pointless.

Ed: Why did the kid bring string to the soccer game?

Ted: He wanted to tie the score.

Macy: Did you hear about the pet store owner who couldn't sell his porcupine?

Lacy: Yeah, he was stuck with it.

Don: Do you know why the guy was fired from the calendar factory?

Ron: He took a day off.

Q: What goes into the water green and comes out blue?

A: A frog on a cold day.

Harper: What's brown, has antlers, and squeaks?

Asher: A moose on a rusty bike.

Q: What do you drop when you need it but take back when you don't?

A: An anchor.

Knock, knock.
Who's there?
Etch.
Etch who?
Gesundheit.

Q: What three letters can frighten a burglar?
A: ICU.

Stan: Did I tell you the construction joke?
Dan: Nope.
Stan: I'm still working on it.

Q: Why did the cow cross the road?

A: To get to the udder side.

Q: What pet makes the loudest noise?

A: A trum-pet.

I couldn't remember how to throw a boomerang. But eventually it came back to me.

I was going to look for my missing watch but I never could find the time.

Q: What does a thesaurus eat for breakfast?

A: A synonym roll.

Jon: How does a dog stop a DVD?
Ron: He hits the paws button.

Bo: How does a mouse feel after a shower?
Jo: Squeaky clean.

Terry: What do you call an elephant in a phone booth?
Mary: Stuck!

Q: What do giant whales eat?
A: Fish and ships.

Q: What do you give a pig with poison oak?
A: Oinkment.

Q: What's a frog's favorite drink?
A: Croaka-Cola.

Alsea: Where do hamburgers go to dance?
Max: The meat ball.

Q: Who makes dinosaur clothes?

A: A dino-sewer.

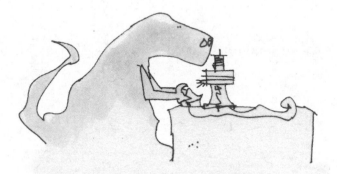

Knock, knock.

Who's there?

Luke.

Luke who?

Luke through the peephole and see for yourself.

Warden: How would you like to celebrate your birthday?

Inmate: What would you think of an open house?

Q: What dinosaur loves to sleep?

A: A Stego-snore-us.

Sam: What do Santa's helpers learn at school?
Pam: The elf-abet.

Q: What kind of lion never roars?

A: A dande-lion.

Q: What runs around a yard but never moves?

A: A fence.

Q: What do you call a bear that flies and never grows up?

A: Peter Panda.

Q: What's an Australian bear's favorite soft drink?

A: Coca-Koala.

Q: Why did the elephant paint himself lots of colors?

A: So he could hide in the crayon box.

Q: How do you know if there's an elephant under your bed?

A: Your head hits the ceiling.

Q: How can you tell if an elephant has been in your refrigerator?

A: From the footprints in the butter.

Q: How can you tell if an elephant has been in your pantry?

A: The peanuts are all gone.

Tongue Twisters

Which Swiss wristwatches are the real Swiss wristwatches?

Cooks cook cupcakes quickly.

Does your sport shop stock short socks with spots?

Chop Imagine shops stock chops.

Imagine an imaginary menagerie manager.

Q: What's gray and goes round and round?

A: An elephant in a dryer.

Q: Why did the elephant float down the river on his back?

A: So he wouldn't get his tennis shoes wet.

Q: Why do elephants wear sandals?

A: So they won't sink in the sand.

Q: Why do ostriches stick their heads in the ground?

A: They're looking for elephants who forgot to wear their sandals.

Hannah: What has four legs, a trunk, and sunglasses?

Deagan: A mouse on vacation.

Q: Where do people go when they have two broken legs?

A: Nowhere.

Donny: What's worse than raining cats and dogs?
Lonny: Hailing taxi cabs.

Max: How do kittens shop?
Jax: They order from cat-alogs.

Q: What do you call it when you paint a picture of your cat's feet?
A: A paw-trait.

Q: What do you call a confused cat?
A: Purr-plexed.

Q: What's a cat's favorite color?
A: Purr-ple.

Q: What's a snake's favorite subject in school?

A: Hissstory.

Ted: What did the teddy bear say after dinner?
Ned: "I'm stuffed!"

The optimist says the glass is half full. The pessimist says the glass is half empty. The mother says, "Why didn't you use a coaster?"

Farmer Brown: What did the mom cow say to the baby cow?

Mrs. Brown: "It's pasture bedtime."

Q: What's a cow's favorite holiday?

A: Moo Year's Day.

Q: What do you call a stampede at a cow ranch?

A: Udder chaos.

Bob: Why did the Secret Service surround the president with cows?

Rob: Because they wanted to beef up security.

Q: What's a cow's favorite type of math?

A: Cow-culus.

Q: What do you get when you cross an angry cow with an annoyed sheep?

A: An animal that's in a baaad mooood.

Q: What's the difference between a dog and a marine biologist?

A: One wags a tail, and the other tags a whale.

Ron: Why did the giant wear a baseball glove?

Jon: He was hoping to catch a bus.

Mason: What's a dog's favorite profession?

Jason: Bark-eology.

Q: Where do the cows eat lunch?

A: In the calf-eteria.

Q: What two things can you never eat for breakfast?

A: Lunch and dinner.

Q: What's gray and beautiful and wears a glass slipper?

A: Cinderella-phant.

Q: What do you get when you cross a Labrador, a poodle, and a magician?

A: A Labracadabradoodle.

Iris: Twenty kids tried to get under one umbrella and, believe it or not, none of them got wet.

Bo: How did that happen?

Iris: It wasn't raining.

Q: What do you call two guys hanging on a window?

A: Kurt and Rod.

Q: What's a bunny's favorite music?

A: Hip-hop.

Mom, what's it like to have the
best daughter in the whole world?

I don't know, dear.
You'll have to ask Grandma.

Tim: Why did the guy get fired from the orange juice factory?

Kim: He couldn't concentrate.

Teacher: Sandy, use the word *rhythm* in a sentence.

Sandy: My brother is going to the movies, and I want to go rhythm.

Aiden: Dad, I've got great news. Remember when you said you'd give me $500 if I got good grades this term?

Dad: Yeah. Sure.

Aiden: Well, you get to keep the money!

Q: What bug arrests all the other bugs?

A: A cop-roach.

Q: What candy do you eat on the playground?

A: Recess Pieces.

Bill: Why couldn't the cookie reach the table?
Phil: Because it was a shortbread.

Knock, knock.

Who's there?

Abbott.

Abbott who?

Abbott you don't know who this is.

Harper: Have you ever seen a catfish?
Asher: No, how does he hold the fishing pole?

Q: What kind of keys do kids like to carry?

A: Cookies!

Q: Where did the kittens go on their school field trip?

A: To the mewseum.

Q: How do bees get to school?

A: On the school buzz of course.

Bill: What happens when it rains cats and dogs?
Jill: You might step in a poodle.

Q: Why did the police hire the duck?
A: They wanted him to quack the case.

Terry: Why did the teacher bring crackers to school?
Jerry: It was parrot-teacher conference day.

Max: Why did the elephant sit on the marshmallow?

Alsea: He didn't want to fall in the hot chocolate.

Q: When does a horse talk?

A: Whinny wants to.

Q: How do bunnies travel?

A: By hareplane.

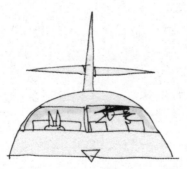

Q: What do you call a bunch of smart trees?

A: A brainforest.

Q: What do you call a guy who owns a truck?

A: Van.

Q: What do you get when you cross a dinosaur with a pig?

A: Jurassic Pork.

Sage Advice: Never argue with a fool; he may be doing the same thing.

Q: What is a pirate's favorite tool?

A: A sea saw.

Q: Why are some fish at the bottom of the ocean?

A: They dropped out of school.

Q: Where is a car most likely to get a flat tire?

A: At a fork in the road.

Mason: Why did the baby strawberry cry?
Jason: Because his folks were in a jam.

Q: What's a gymnast's favorite season?

A: Spring.

Q: How is a baseball team similar to a muffin?

A: They both depend on the batter.

Q: What do firefighters put in their soup?

A: Firecrackers.

Q: Why was the broom late for class?

A: It overswept.

Bo: Why did the girl bring lipstick and eye shadow to class?

Iris: She had a makeup exam.

When I see a cookie, I hear two voices in my head. One says, "You need to eat that cookie." The other one says, "You heard him, eat that cookie."

Bus Driver (to passenger): Don't you want to take a seat?

Passenger: No thanks. I already have enough to carry.

Misty: What's the name of your new dog?

Christy: I don't know; he won't tell me.

Q: Why didn't the hatchet go to the party?

A: It wasn't axed.

Caden: Do you know how to keep a dummy in suspense?

Braeden: No, how?

Caden: I'll tell you tomorrow.

Q: What's red and orange and knocks you over?

A: Tackle Me Elmo.

Teacher: Carlos, go to the map and point to North America.

Carlos: (*Points to the map.*) Here it is.

Teacher: Good job! Now, class, who discovered North America?

Class: Carlos!

Ted: Where do you put smart hot dogs?

Ned: On honor rolls!

Q: Where do crayons go on vacation?

A: Color-ado!

Q: What do you call a funny chicken?

A: A comedi-hen.

Wife: Doctor, you've got to help us. For five years, my husband has been convinced he's a chicken.

Doctor: Why didn't you call me earlier?

Wife: We needed the eggs.

Asher: What do you call it when you have Grandma on speed dial?

Bo: Insta-Gram.

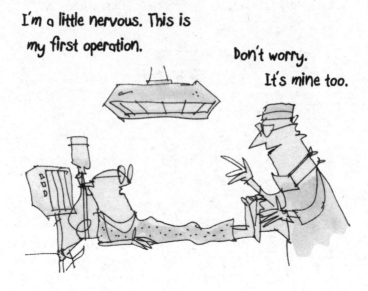

Jan: Why did the boy take a pencil to his bedroom?

Dan: He wanted to draw the curtains.

Q: What do you call a bee who's having a bad hair day?

A: A Frizzbee.

Did you hear about the paddle sale at the boat store?
It was quite an oar-deal.

Did you hear about the limo driver who didn't have a customer for 25 years?

He worked all that time and had nothing to chauffer it.

Tongue Twisters

A box of mixed biscuits, a mixed biscuit box.

The sixth sick sheik's sixth sick sheep.

What time does the wristwatch strap shop shut?

Flash message! Flash message!

Six thick sticky thistle sticks.

Why do you drive on a parkway but park on a driveway?

Knock, knock.

Who's there?

Scott.

Scott who?

Scott nothing to do with you.

Q: Why can you never go hungry at the beach?

A: You can always eat the sand which is there.

Teacher: Rylie, which hand do you like to write with?
Rylie: Neither. I like to use a pencil.

Q: What did one rubber band say to the other rubber band?

A: "Snap out of it!"

Q: What do pigs use to write a letter?

A: A pigpen.

Hal: What do you give a baker's daughter on your first date?

Sal: Flours.

Q: What did the police officer say to his sweater?

A: "Do you know why I pulled you over?"

Q: Why did the baker work overtime?

A: He kneaded the dough.

Q: Why did the belt get arrested?

A: Because it held up a pair of pants.

Donny: Where do birds invest their money?

Lonny: In the stork market.

Q: What are caterpillars afraid of?

A: Dogger-pillars.

Q: What do you call a bear who's caught in the rain?

A: A drizzly bear.

> **Dad:** What did you learn in school today?
> **Kid:** They taught us how to write.
> **Dad:** Wow, what did you write?
> **Kid:** I don't know; they haven't taught us how to read yet.

Q: What did the baby corn say to the mama corn?

A: "Where's Pop?"

I used to be indecisive. Now I'm not so sure.

Sam: Dad, I got a *D* in math.

Dad: Well, what are we going to do?

Sam: For one thing, I need you to stop doing my homework.

Ditzy Girl: My father flew in for the weekend.

Friend: Oh, how nice. Did you meet him at the airport?

Ditzy Girl: Oh no, I've known him all my life.

Q: What do you call a web page for an optometrist?

A: A site for sore eyes.

Husband: Happy Birthday! Remember that bright red Porsche you've always wanted?

Wife: Why yes, dear.

Husband: Good, 'cause I got you a toothbrush in the exact same color!

Q: Where do horses go shopping?

A: Old Neighvy.

I got fired from my job in the kitchen for stealing utensils. It was a whisk I was willing to take.

Teacher: Be sure you go straight home.

    Boy: I can't. I live around the corner.

Q: What did the big bucket say to the small bucket?

A: "You look a little pail."

    Terry: Why did the policeman bring a jar of peanut butter to the freeway?

    Jerry: He heard there was a traffic jam.

Q: What do you get when you cross a rabbit with a frog?

A: A bunny ribbit.

Did you hear about the postal worker who was upset?
He got mad and stamped his feet.

Q: What's the world's largest punctuation mark?

A: The 100-yard dash.

Mason: What do you call a dinosaur who's at the bottom
of the sea?

Jason: A Tyrannosaurus Wreck.

Rod: Why is tennis such a loud game?

Todd: Because all the players raise a racket.

Hey, lower the racket down there!

Q: What's the tallest piece of furniture?

A: A bookcase. It's got the most stories.

Movie Ticket Seller: I'm sorry. We're all sold out—right down to the last seat.

> **Customer:** Great! I'll take the last seat, please.

Q: What do you get when you cross a carrier pigeon with a parrot?

A: A carrier pigeon who stops to ask for directions.

Q: Why did the chicken cross the playground?

A: To get to the other slide.

Q: What's yellow and goes "Ho, ho, ho"?

A: Santa Banana.

Bill: Somebody robbed the bakery yesterday.

Jill: Well, doesn't that take the cake!

Randy: I've forgotten everything I've ever learned.
Andy: Well, what do you know!

Ron: Why did Alice wear only one boot?
Jon: She heard the snow was one foot deep.

Max: What's worse than being with a fool?
Jax: Fooling with a bee.

Knew a lady who loved a bargain. She bought everything that was marked down. Last week she brought home an elevator.

Mason: Where do sharks go on vacation?
Jason: Finland.

Teacher: Joey, where can you find the Red Sea?

Joey: Usually on my report card.

City Guy: How do you stop moles from digging in your garden?

Farmer: Easy. Hide the shovel.

Scientist 1: I see your microscope magnifies three times.

Scientist 2: Oh rats! I've used it twice already!

Judge: You have a choice: 30 days in jail or $100.

Convict: I'll take the money!

Q: What did the nut say when it sneezed?

A: "Cashew!"

Sue: Why does Philip jump up and down before drinking his chocolate milk?

Fred: Because the carton says, "Shake well before using."

Q: Why won't the shrimp share his lunch?

A: 'Cause he's a little shellfish.

Q: What's a small dog's favorite soft drink?

A: Pupsi-Cola.

Q: What is flat and golden brown and doesn't want to grow up?

A: Peter Pancake.

Kid: I can't figure out this math problem.

Teacher: Are you serious? Any five-year-old can figure that out!

Kid: Well, no wonder. I'm eight.

Q: Where do sea otters keep their space station?

A: In otter space.

Have you heard about the new movie about a fruit farmer?
It's rated Peachy-13.

Q: What's big and gray and has horns?

A: An elephant marching band.

Doctor: What seems to be the trouble?

Patient: I keep thinking that no one can hear me.

Doctor: What seems to be the trouble?

Q: What do you get when you cross a small bear with a skunk?

A: Winnie the Pew.

Q: Where do ducks look up words?

A: In the duck-tionary.

Q: What's a hog's favorite game?

A: Pig-pong.

Ron: How can you tell if there's an elephant in your peanut butter?

Don: Check the list of ingredients.

Q: Where do mice go while wearing costumes?

A: A mousequerade party.

Patient: Doctor, I'm convinced I'm a needle and thread!
Doctor: How do you feel?
Patient: Sew-sew.

Man: Doctor, I think I'm a parachute!
Doctor: Call me next week when I have an opening.

Q: What has 100 feet and says, "Ho, ho, ho"?

A: A Santa-pede.

Man: Doctor, I'm convinced I'm a smoke detector.

Doctor: Don't worry. There's no cause for alarm.

Q: What's a pig's favorite winter Olympic sport?

A: Ice hoggy.

Hans: Where do old Vikings live?

Swen: In Norse-ing homes.

Patient: Doctor, I'm convinced I'm an umbrella!

Doctor: Oh, you must be under the weather.

Man: Doctor, I'm convinced I'm a bridge!

Doctor: Oh my, what's come over you?

Man: So far, two trucks and a bus.

Bob: What do you get when you cross a parrot with a pig?

Rob: A loud bird that hogs the conversation.

Policeman: Your dog was seen chasing a family in a car.

Pet Owner: Don't be ridiculous. My dog doesn't even know how to drive.

Knock, knock.

Who's there?

Figs.

Figs who?

Figs the doorbell. It's broken!

Q: What's purple and conquers foreign lands?

A: Alexander the Grape.

Q: What do you call a huge herd of giraffes on the freeway?

A: A giraffic jam.

Customer: May I speak to the head boomerang
salesman?
Receptionist: I'm sorry. Can he get back to you?

Did you hear about the guy who fell into an upholstery
machine?
Don't worry. He's fully recovered now.

Bo: Hey, I heard you failed your karate test.
Asher: Yeah, I could kick myself.

A guy was observing two city workers in a park. One would
dig a hole and the other would quickly fill it in. He finally
asked what they were doing.
"Normally there are three of us. One guy plants the tree,
but he's out sick today."

Mom, everyone
in town says
I'm a liar!

I find that hard to believe.

Patient: I'm always dizzy for a half hour when I get up in the morning. What should I do?

Doctor: Try getting up a half hour later.

Did you hear about the pancake chef who became an air traffic controller?

Now he's got planes stacked up all over the country.

I've got too many planes lined up! How waffle!

Piano Player: Do you think I have a gift for playing?

Listener: I don't know, but I'll give you one for stopping.

Q: Where do cows go on vacation?

A: To Cowlifornia.

Q: What do you call a guy who's hung on the wall?

A: Art.

Rocket Scientist: We are planning a rocket trip like no other. We are going to fly to the sun!

Reporter: That's ridiculous. You'll burn up as soon as you get near it!

Rocket Scientist: Ah ha! That's why we're going at night!

Navy Recruiter: Do you know how to swim?

Recruit: Why, aren't there enough ships?

Tongue Twisters

Give Papa a proper cup of coffee in a copper coffee cup.

Nat's knapsack strap snapped.

You know you need unique New York.

Bad money, mad bunny.

Stick strictly six stick stumps.

Ron: Are you going out with the librarian Saturday night?

Don: No, she was already booked.

Diner: What's this fly doing in my ice cream?

Waiter: Probably cooling off. It gets pretty hot in the soup.

Judge: Do you plead guilty or not guilty?

Convict: I don't know; I haven't heard the evidence yet.

Customer: I'm looking for a new mattress.

Salesman: Do you want a spring mattress?

Customer: No thanks. I need one I can use all year.

Salesman: Would you like to buy a pocket calculator?

Customer: No thanks. I already know how many pockets I have.

Jon: I heard you got a job as a trash collector.

Ron: Yeah, I don't know much about it, but I figure I'll pick it up as I go along.

Teacher: Johnny, can you name the four seasons?

Johnny: Sure. Salt, pepper, vinegar, and mustard!

Teacher: Conner, how fast does light travel?

Conner: I don't know, but it gets here way too early in the morning.

Man at the Door: I'm here to tune your piano.
Piano Student: But I didn't send for you.
Man: No, but your neighbors did.

Manager: You can't help admiring our boss.
New Employee: Why is that?
Manager: 'Cause if you don't, you're fired.

Asher: I just rode the carousel 15 times.
Harper: Wow! You sure do get around, don't you?

Logan: This ointment makes my leg smart.
Rogan: Why don't you try rubbing it on your head?

Diner: Give me a spaghetti sandwich on rye.
Waiter: That's crazy! Nobody orders a spaghetti sandwich on rye!
Diner: You're right. Make it on whole wheat.

Patient: Doctor, I can't seem to get to sleep at night.

Doctor: Well, lie on the edge of the bed, and soon you'll just drop right off.

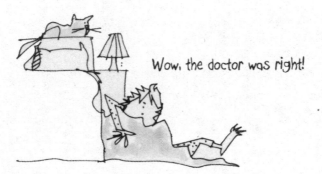

Wow, the doctor was right!

Police Captain: The thief got away, huh? Did you guard all the exits?

Patrolman: Yeah, we sure did, but he snuck out one of the entrances!

Jon: Why are you putting a bandage on your paycheck?

Ron: I just got a cut in my salary.

Bride: Darling, we've been married for 24 hours!
Groom: Yes, dear, it seems like only yesterday!

Mary: I'm going to take a milk bath.
Shari: Pasteurized?
Mary: No, just up to my shoulders.

Customer: I'd like a ticket to New York State, please.
Ticket Agent: Would you like to go by Buffalo?
Customer: No thanks. I'd rather take the bus.

Two construction workers were having lunch outside their work site.

First Guy: Oh no, not again! A peanut butter sandwich. I can't stand it! Day in and day out, always a peanut butter sandwich. This is too much!

Second Guy: Why don't you ask your wife to make you something different?

First Guy: I can't do that.

Second Guy: Why not?

First Guy: I make my own lunch!

Diner: This pea soup tastes like detergent!

Waiter: Oh, that must be the chicken soup. The pea soup tastes like gasoline.

Performer: Do you think my singing is becoming?
Audience Member: Yes, it's becoming annoying.

A scientist crossed poison ivy with a four-leaf clover and got a rash of good luck.

Mason: Do you have trouble making up your mind?
Jason: Well, yes and no.

Tim: Do you like your new job in the rubber band factory?
Jim: Oh, it's a snap.

Rick: A guy sold me the Nile River for $200.
Nick: Egypt you.

Doctor: You need glasses!
Patient: I already have glasses.
Doctor: Then *I* need glasses!

Q: Who steals accessories off of cars and gives them to the poor?

A: Robin Hood Ornament.

Remy: I'll give you $500 if you do the worrying for me.
Ava: Where's the $500?
Remy: That's your first worry.

Sir, there's a man outside
holding a drum.

Tell him to beat it.

Captain: Sailor, did you clean the ship as ordered?

Sailor: Yes sir! I swabbed the deck, I cleaned the portholes, and I even swept the horizon with my telescope.

Professor: I'm studying ancient history.

Teaching Assistant: Me too. Let's get together and talk about old times.

Don: I wish I had enough money to buy an elephant.

Ron: Why would you want an elephant?

Don: I don't. I just want the money.

Diner: Is this peach or apple pie?

Waiter: Can't you tell by the taste?

Diner: No, I can't.

Waiter: Well then, what difference does it make?

Q: Why did the boy take his crayons to the zoo?

A: He wanted to try coloring outside the lions.

Q: What does a lawyer wear to work?

A: A law suit.

Kid: A man came by to see you.

Mom: Did he have a bill?

Kid: No, just a regular nose.

Donny: Every night I take two 25-cent pieces to bed with me.

Lonny: What for?

Donny: They're my sleeping quarters.

Q: What's an astronaut's favorite food?

A: Launch meat!

Hannah: My new radio is so powerful that last night I got Mexico.

Deagan: So what? Last night I just opened my window and got Chile.

Did you hear about the guy who stole a truck filled with rubber bands?

He was put away for a long stretch.

Q: What do you call a chicken crossing the road?

A: Poultry in motion.

Ann: What do you get when you cross a maid with a giraffe?

Fran: I don't know, but my ceilings have never been cleaner!

Q: Why did the elephant stay home from the beach?

A: He couldn't find his trunks.

Q: What does the astronaut use to serve dinner?

A: A satellite dish.

Conner: Last night I slept on a 10-foot bed!

Chloe: That's a lot of bunk.

Q: How did the llama get to the movie premiere?

A: He went in a llamasine.

Q: Why did the stegosaurus need a bandage?

A: He had a dino-sore.

Q: Why did the forgetful lady go for a run?

A: She wanted to jog her memory.

Q: Why did the muffler quit the car business?

A: He was exhausted.

Knock, knock.

Who's there?

Classify.

Classify who?

Classify don't give you any homework, will you all pay attention?

Knock, knock.

Who's there?

Trainee.

Trainee who?

Trainee was trying to catch left 10 minutes ago.

Q: How do you write a note at the beach?

A: You use sandpaper.

Knock, knock.

Who's there?

Wafer.

Wafer who?

Wafer me. I'm almost ready.

Q: Where do bees go on vacation?

A: Stingapore.

Q: What do you call a deer in the car shouting directions?

A: A buck-seat driver.

Turn left here! No, no, the next street! Aren't you going a little fast? Slow down!

Knock, knock.

Who's there?

Apollo G.

Apollo G. who?

Apollo G. accepted.

Knock, knock.

Who's there?

Diploma.

Diploma who?

Diploma is here to fix da bathtub.

Knock, knock.

Who's there?

Huron.

Huron who?

Huron my foot. Ouch!

Knock, knock.

Who's there?

Tank.

Tank who?

You're welcome.

Knock, knock.

Who's there?

Dots.

Dots who?

Dots for me to know and you to find out.

Knock, knock.

Who's there?

Wire.

Wire who?

Wire you asking?

Q: What does a farmer give his wife for Valentine's Day?

A: Hogs and kisses.

Q: What does a French chef give his wife for Valentine's Day?

A: Hugs and quiches.

Q: What did one pickle say to the other?

A: "You mean a great dill to me."

A little girl was at her first wedding. She leaned over to her mom and whispered, "Why did the lady change her mind?"

"What do you mean, honey?"

"Well, she came down the aisle with one man and left with another."

Tongue Twister

Betty Botter bought some butter, but she said, "This butter's bitter. If I put it in my batter, it will make my batter bitter." So she bought a bit of butter, better than the bitter butter.

Man: Doctor, you've got to help me. I'm convinced I'm a doorbell.

Doctor: Well, take two aspirins and give me a ring in the morning.

Mike: What school do you have to drop out of to graduate from?

Ike: Parachute school!

Yeah, looks like they broke
in and stole everything but
the soap, the shampoo, and
the towels.

Those dirty crooks.

Conner: Why did the boy take a ruler to bed?

Chloe: He wanted to see how long he slept.

Q: Where do eggs go on vacation?

A: New Yolk City.

Jon: Why was the guy fired from the automobile assembly line?

Ron: He was caught taking a brake.

Chad: What sits at the bottom of the ocean and shakes?

Rad: A nervous wreck.

Four out of three people have problems with fractions.

Harper: Why won't the mummy go on vacation?

Iris: He's afraid he might relax and unwind.

Q: What did Delaware?

A: A New Jersey.

Neighbor: Why are you wearing all those jackets while you're painting your house?

Fran: The paint can said to put on three coats.

The forecast is clear and 60 degrees
with a 70% chance we're wrong.

Q: What do you get when you cross a cactus with a bicycle?

A: A flat tire.

Terry: Why are elephants so wrinkled?
Jerry: 'Cause they're almost impossible to iron.

Q: What is red, then yellow, then red, then yellow?

A: An apple that works part time as a banana.

Teacher: Tommy, can you use the word *aftermath* in a sentence?
Tommy: Sure. Aftermath class is over, I can go home.

Q: Why did the boy stay on the merry-go-round for three straight days?

A: He was trying to set a whirled record.

I bought a dictionary yesterday, but when I got home all the pages were blank. I don't have the words to describe how upset I am.

Q: Why do hens lay eggs?

A: 'Cause if they threw them, they'd break!

I stayed up all night wondering where the sun was. Then it dawned on me.

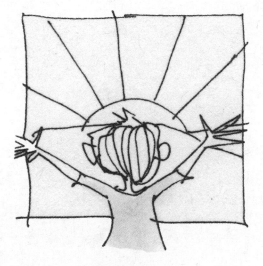

Kylie: What does the horse say to the guy who lives next door?

   Iris: "Hay, neeeiiggghhh-bor."

Q: How can you tell if there's an elephant in your bedroom?

A: By the big *E* on his pajamas.

Q: What do dogs like to eat at the movies?

A: Pup-corn.

Old Lady: Son, can you help me across the street?

    Scout: Okay, but I can help you right here just as well.

    Jo: Does February March?

    Bo: Well, April May.

    Stan: Did you hear the one about the three holes in the ground?

    Dan: No, tell me.

    Stan: Well, well, well.

Q: What kind of photos do turtles take?

A: Shellfies!

Q: Who was the roundest knight at King Arthur's Round Table?

A: Sir Cumference.

Guy in the Library: I'll have a cheeseburger and fries.

Librarian: Sir, you know this is a library.

Guy: Oh, sorry. (*Whispers*) I'll have a cheeseburger and fries.

More of Emily Biddle's Book Titles:

Here are some more interesting book titles from Emily's bookmobile:

The Ball Game Will Go On by Raynor Shine

Use Those Credit Cards! by Bill Melater

Italian Cooking by Liz Anya

Join the Band! by Clara Nett

I'm So Stuffed by Ada Lotte

I Was Robbed by Alma Money

Where Are All the Cookies? by Arthur Anymore

Everything You Need to Know about Explosives by Dinah Mite

My Adventures in Space by Andy Gravity

I'm Unemployed by Anita Jobb

Living with Robots by Ann Droid

Give Your Car a Tune-Up by Carl Humm

Where to Keep Your Plants by Clay Potts

Handling Dynamite by E. Z. Duzzett

Flips, Handstands, and Somersaults by Jim Nastics

How to Volunteer by Linda Hand

The Flooded Bathroom by Lee King Fawcett

Make Your Yard Look Great by Moe D. Lawn

Get Your Eyes Checked by Seymour Clearly

Sandy Silverthorne, author of *Crack Yourself Up Jokes for Kids, More Crack Yourself Up Jokes for Kids, Made You Laugh!*, and *Now That's Funny*, has been writing and illustrating books since 1988 and currently has over 800,000 copies in print. His award-winning Great Bible Adventure children's series with Harvest House sold over 170,000 copies and has been distributed in eight languages worldwide. His One-Minute Mysteries series has sold over 240,000 copies. He's written and illustrated over 30 books and has worked with such diverse clients as Universal Studios Tour, Doubleday Publishers, Penguin, World Vision, the University of Oregon, the Charlotte Hornets, and the Academy of Television Arts and Sciences. Sandy has worked as a cartoonist, author, illustrator, actor, pastor, speaker, and comedian. Apparently, it's hard for him to focus. Connect with him at sandysilverthornebooks.com.

More from
Sandy Silverthorne

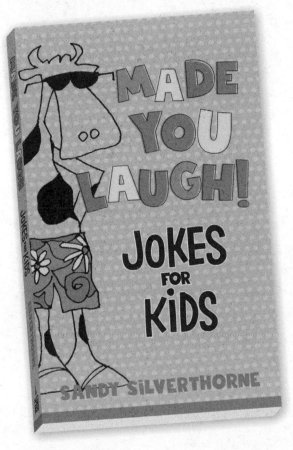

Get ready for hours of fun making your friends laugh,
making your family laugh, but mostly making
yourself laugh! Ideal for kids ages 6–12.

Keep on laughing!

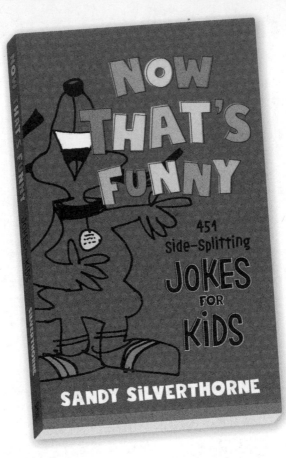

I keep telling people about the benefits of eating dried grapes. It's all about raisin awareness.

Knock, knock.
Who's there?
Spell.
Spell who?
Okay, W-H-O.

Packed full of one-liners, riddles, knock-knock jokes, and hilarious cartoons, *Now That's Funny* will keep you cracking up for days!